S0-AYZ-324

OREGON COAST

portrait of a place

OREGON COAST
portrait of a place

RICK SCHAFER

GRAPHIC ARTS™ BOOKS

All photographs © MMVIII by Rick Schafer
Captions © MMVIII by Graphic Arts™ Books

All rights reserved. No part of this book may be reproduced or
transmitted in any form or by any means, electronic or mechanical,
including photocopying, recording, or by any information storage
and retrieval system, without written permission of the publisher.

Library of Congress Control Number: 2007943515
International Standard Book Number: 978-0-88240-734-0

Book compilation © MMVIII by
Graphic Arts™ Books, an imprint of
Graphic Arts Center Publishing Company
P.O. Box 10306, Portland, Oregon 97296-0306
503/226-2402; www.gacpc.com

The five-dot logo is a registered trademark of
Graphic Arts Center Publishing Company.

President: Charles M. Hopkins
Associate Publisher: Douglas A. Pfeiffer
Editorial Staff: Timothy W. Frew, Kathy Howard, Jean Bond-Slaughter
Production Coordinator: Vicki Knapton
Cover Design: Elizabeth Watson
Interior Design: Jean Andrews

Printed in the United States of America

FRONT COVER: ◖ Rising some hundred feet
above the ocean, the sandstone cliffs of Cape Kiwanda
highlight one of the two famous Oregon coast monoliths
named "Haystack Rock," this one a mile offshore from Pacific City.
BACK COVER: ◖ The Heceta Head Lighthouse was first lit in 1894.
The assistant keeper's house, built in 1893, is now a bed-and-breakfast.
◀◀ A wave crashes against the rocks. Many people love to go to the
beach just to watch the waves—and storms are the greatest attraction of all.
◀ People join seagulls at low tide searching for whatever the sea left behind
on Cannon Beach near The Needles and 235-foot-high Haystack Rock.
▶ Afternoon light and shadow outline intricate designs on
the sand dunes and sea stacks at Cape Sebastian.

◄ Starfish (not truly a fish) and common
blue mussel cling to the rocks near Cannon Beach. If a
starfish loses an arm, it has the ability to regenerate a new one.
▲ Neahkahnie Mountain offers a stunning view of
Manzanita Beach, surf, and blue sky.

▲ Sunrise backlights a barn in Tillamook County.
► Dairy farming is an important part of the economy
on the northern Oregon coast. Each June, the county celebrates
Dairy Month with one of Oregon's largest parades,
averaging almost 150 parade entries.

◄ One of the biggest sand-castle contests organized
on the West Coast, Sandcastle Day is open to everyone
from "Sand Fleas" age six and under to adult "Sand Masters."

▲ Crescent Beach is a jewel of Ecola State Park, which encompasses
approximately 1,300 acres and is an official whale-watching site.

►► A trail leads to the beach at Hug Point State Recreation Area.

11

▲ Open to visitors year-round, the
Tillamook Cheese Factory, a farmer-owned
cooperative, has been producing cheese since 1909.
▶ Visitors enjoy seeing how Tillamook Cheese is
made as well as tasting the finished product.

14

◄ The sun sets behind offshore
rocks at Ecola State Park's Crescent Beach.
▲ Houses are built up the steep hillside at Oceanside,
on the northern Oregon coast.

▲ Fort Clatsop was the winter
encampment for the Lewis & Clark
Expedition from December 1805 to March 1806.
▶ A tree stump creates its own art at Fort Clatsop.
▶▶ A man enjoys watching a boisterous
sea at Fort Stevens State Park.

◄ Cascade Head provides a
stunning view of the Salmon River
estuary. As saltwater mixes with fresh, conditions
become ideal for a wide variety of sea life and their young.
▲ Both sky and sea conspire to highlight rocky outcrops
just offshore from Ecola State Park.

▲ Hotel rooms line this stretch of Cannon Beach.
All along the coast, such places are popular, as people
want to be able to watch the waves—especially during a storm.
► Fishing and pleasure boats dock at Astoria Harbor.

◄ The Nehalem River, 115 miles long, drains
some 855 square miles of the northern Coast Range.
▲ Ferns line the banks of a small creek in Clatsop County.
►► Kids fish off the dock at Coffenbury Lake.

◄ A sea stack in the Three Capes
area (Cape Meares, Cape Lookout, and
Cape Kiwanda) leaves a reflection in the wet sand.
▲ Following a long-held tradition in Cannon Beach,
colorful hanging baskets decorate dozens of shops,
along with porches and lamp posts.

▲ LEFT TO RIGHT: ● The Astoria Column towers 125 feet.
● The Column commemorates the history of Astoria from the
discovery of the Columbia River by Captain Robert Gray, through the
Lewis & Clark Expedition, to the arrival of the Great Northern Railway.
▶ In 1898, a cannon from the USS *Shark*, which ran aground in 1846, was
discovered near today's Cannon Beach, thus the town's name. In 2008, two
more cannons were discovered nearby that may be from the same ship.

◄ Before roads were constructed in the
area, horse-drawn buggies and cars used the beach
as a highway. This rough "road" was carved out of the
rock at Hug Point to make continued travel possible.
▲ Neahkahnie Mountain rises 1,680 feet above sea
level, well above the fog that has rolled in below.

◄ The *Orion* rests at dock in the
shadow of the Astoria Bridge on a foggy day.
▲ In Seaside, a statue of Meriwether Lewis and William
Clark, created in 1990 by sculptor Stanley Wanlass,
marks the official end of the Lewis & Clark Trail.

◄ Cape Meares National Wildlife Refuge protects
remnants of coastal old-growth forest, including Sitka spruce
and western hemlock, and provides habitat for threatened bird species.
▲ The Lightship *Columbia* WLV 604 served near the mouth of
the Columbia River from 1951 to 1979. It now rests at the
Columbia River Maritime Museum in Astoria.

▲ The Columbia River pilot boat MV *Chinook* goes beneath the
Astoria Bridge on a foggy day. The four-mile truss bridge spans the
Columbia from Oregon to Washington. The *Chinook* is designed not
only to survive rough water but also is able to right itself if it overturns.

▶ Barely visible in sunset's light, the Tillamook Lighthouse was
commissioned in 1878, with a budget of $50,000. By the time
the light was finished in 1881, it had cost $125,000.

◄ Fisherman's Pier stretches out into the bay at
Garibaldi, in Tillamook County on Oregon's north coast.
▲ Fogarty Creek State Recreation Area, where Fogarty
Creek meets the Pacific Ocean, is a favorite place
for bird-watching and tide pooling.

◄ Seal Rock State Recreation Site,
south of Newport, encompasses large offshore
rock formations, which are habitat for seals and sea lions.
▲ The inside stairway of the Umpqua River Lighthouse spirals up
to the light sixty-five feet above. Constructed 165 feet above
sea level, the light can be seen for more than twenty
miles. It is the only red lens on the West Coast.

◄ Fishing nets and geraniums
mark a marina on the Siuslaw River.
▲ Early morning fog surrounds pilings and
a marina near Florence at the mouth
of the Siuslaw River.

47

▲ LEFT TO RIGHT: ● There is no such thing as a "horrible day at the beach" as penned by Keith Robinson at the Oregon Coast Aquarium. Blue skies, stormy skies, tranquil waves, or boisterous—the coast always invites. ● Part of the Passages of the Deep exhibit, the Open Sea passage ends with a replica of the jaws of a megalodon, a giant prehistoric shark also sometimes called a megatooth shark.

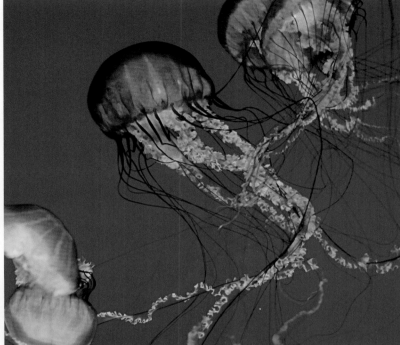

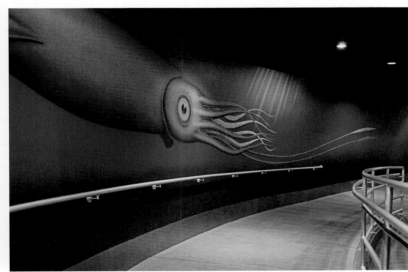

▲ CLOCKWISE FROM TOP LEFT:
The Oregon Coast Aquarium protects more than just fish:
● Adult snowy plover, an endangered species, care for orphaned babies;
● Jellyfish move gracefully; ● a giant squid greets visitors; and
● Sea anemones add their bright colors.

▲ The Yaquina Bay Harbor holds the reflection of
the Yaquina Bay Bridge. The arch bridge has spanned
the bay since its completion in 1936, at a cost of $1,301,016.

▶ Some say the name *Yachats* comes from the Siletz language, and
means "dark waters at the foot of the mountain." The way homes are built
down the mountain to the very edge of the ocean reinforces the name.

▶▶ A man shares clamming with seabirds at Salishan's Siletz Bay.

◄ The forest meets the sea at Cape Perpetua.
At its crest eight hundred feet above sea level, an
observer can see seventy miles of Oregon coastline.
▲ Mo's Restaurant is a staple of Old Town Newport.
Next door in the same building, arrangements
can be made for a deep-sea fishing adventure.

▲ At ninety-six feet high,
the Yaquina Bay Lighthouse, built
in 1871, is the tallest on the Oregon coast.
▶ Newport Harbor presents a tranquil
scene in early morning.

◄ The wide blue sky is one of the attractions of the coast.
▲ One way to enjoy that blue sky is with kites—shown here at Catch
the Wind Kites in Newport. Kite festivals—both indoor and outdoor—
attract people from all over the world to Oregon's central coast.

◄ Morning mist floats above a
sunlit Devils Lake, near Lincoln City.
▲ Crab pots in Newport await use. Dungeness
and Japanese red rock crab attract
crabbers all along the coast.

▲ The Devil's Punch Bowl is a rock formation
probably created when the roof of a cave collapsed,
leaving a bowl-shaped depression behind. The name
comes from the way waves fill the "bowl" and swirl around.
▶ ALL IMAGES: Waves of all kinds—gentle and flowing,
rough and stormy, crashing through holes in rocks—
attract thousands to the coast each year.

◄ Water rushes over the rocks at
Bob Creek Wayside. The Wayside teems
with tide pools full of fascinating bits of sea life.
▲ The Bay Street Pier in Newport offers shopping along
with ever-changing views of the oceanfront.

▲ A sunset view of Heceta Head Lighthouse
points out the challenges faced in 1892 in planning
to build a lighthouse on a hillside 205 feet above the water.
► The town of Yachats, in Lincoln County, is famous for its ocean views.
►► An unusual beach composed of polished black rocks marks
Yaquina Head Outstanding Natural Area.

▲ The Rogue Ales Public House, originally called
the Bayfront Brewery, first opened its doors in 1989.
▶ At night, the Newport waterfront is still a busy place,
the lights along the water lending a romantic air.

◄ Colorful poppies and cosmos
carpet a hillside in Honeyman State Park.
▲ The mighty blue Pacific Ocean stretches out
from this vantage point at Cape Perpetua.

▲ Fishing boats have come home
to rest in front of the town of Florence.
► Lakes and sandtraps add to the difficulty of the
eighteenth green at Sandpines Golf Course in Florence.
►► A lazy Pacific surf rolls into Devils Elbow
State Park, near Florence.

▲ Cummins Creek flows through
Neptune State Park, near Yachats. The park is a great
place to watch for whales, sea lions, and even an occasional deer.
► Breakers smash into the rocks at Shore Acres State Park.

◄ The scenic cove where Fogerty Creek meets the
ocean is sheltered from the wind by a headland blanketed
with Sitka spruce, western hemlock, shore pine, and alder forest.
▲ Huge rocks stick up from the beach at Bandon State
Natural Area as the waves roll ashore.

▲ The first U.S. Lifesaving Service station opened at
South Beach in 1895. Today, U.S. Coast Guard Station
Yaquina Bay is given the responsibility of search
and rescue, as well as law enforcement.

▲ Within sight of the Yaquina Bay Bridge,
sea lions have found a different use for a boat dock—
it's apparently a great place to haul out and bask in the sun.
►► Coastal forest cloaks the banks of the Millicoma River.

▲ Bandon Dunes Golf Resort, situated just north
of Bandon, incorporates three golf courses. This one,
Bandon Dunes, was designed by Scotsman David McLay Kidd.
▶ Highway 101 meets the shoreline near Cape Sebastian.

◄ Flowering gorse decorates
the shoreline above a rock-studded
Bandon Beach on the southern Oregon coast.
▲ Wind has etched ripple patterns into the
sand at Pistol River State Park.

▲ Cranberries have been grown in Coos
and Curry counties since 1885. Early Dutch and
German settlers called it "crane berry," which was
later shortened to "cranberry." The cranberry is
a major crop on the southern Oregon coast.

▲ Barnacles and starfish cling
to the jagged edges of sea stacks near Cape
Sebastian. The cape was named in 1603 in honor of
Saint Sebastian by Spanish navigator Sebastian Vizcaino.
▶▶ The Coast Guard dredge *Yaquina* helps keep entrance
bars, rivers, and harbors clear so international freighters
can bring their wares to Oregon's ports.

▲ Sea stacks dot the shoreline of Harris
Beach in southern Oregon's Curry County.
► The fishing vessel *Darin Alan* is
docked at Gold Beach.

◄ The Winchuck is the southern-
most river on the Oregon coast, meeting the
sea less than a mile north of the California border.
▲ A couple play in the water at Sunset Bay State Park.
Protected by towering sea cliffs, the sandy beaches at
Sunset Bay invite a variety of water play, including
swimming, boating, and beachcombing.

97

▲ People enjoy climbing on the rocks at Shore
Acres State Park, but safety precautions are essential.
► Although sea lions are found in a number of colonies
situated along the Oregon coast, one of the most popular places
to see them is at the Sea Lion Caves near Florence.
►► The setting sun outlines sea stacks at
Bandon State Natural Area.

◄ A moss-draped tree leans over the waters of the
Millicoma River, a large northern tributary of the Coos River.
▲ A lone purple wild iris pokes through a bed of trillium.

▲ In Port Orford, the *Rosalie* waits
to be lifted into the water by the West Coast's
only dolly-and-crane system.

▲ The Coquille River Lighthouse at the
mouth of the Coquille River was completed
in 1886; it provided continuous protection
for ships entering the river until 1963
when it was decommissioned.

▲ The Isaac Lee Patterson Bridge crosses the Rogue
River, connecting the towns of Wedderburn and Gold Beach.
The area is a popular place for salmon fishing, crabbing, and boat trips.
▶ BOTH IMAGES: Whale watching is a favorite pastime of young and old alike
all along the Oregon coast. Whale-watching cruises are a great way to see a whale close-up.
▶▶ Sunlight sparkles on the water as a fog bank threatens to roll in and obliterate it all.

▲ A pink tint fills the sky above Shore Acres
State Park and the Cape Arago Lighthouse, which
protected ships from the rocky shoreline from 1934 to 2006.
► The Pacific surf continues to shape and smooth the
huge sandstone cliffs of Shore Acres State Park.
►► A colorful sunset silhouettes Haystack
Rock at Cannon Beach.

110